ADVANCED STUDIES

JULIUS WEISSENBORN
Adapted by
William E. Rhoads

Allegro moderato - With full tone

Allegretto - risoluto

B-256

Allegro assai

5.

poco f

rit. - - - - - - - - - a tempo

cresc. - - - - - - - - - - - - - -

poco f

3

4

SCHERZO

6

Allegretto

9.

Allegro moderato

10.

Allegro

14.

mf

Tempo di marcia

16.

14

SCHERZO
Allegro vivace

B-256

Allegretto

21.

Andante con moto quasi allegro moderato

22.

Andante quasi allegretto

25.

Allegro ma non troppo

26.

Allegro moderato

29.

Allegro vivace

30.

Adagio di molto

31.

Tema con variazioni

Intrada

Andante

33.